D1004175

Risk-Taking in Learning, K-3

The Author

Robert D. Young is Assistant Professor of Early Childhood Education at the University of North Alabama, Florence.

The Advisory Panel

Linda Carlson Armstrong, Teacher, Department of Defense Dependents Schools, Torrejon Air Base, Spain

Kathryn Blomquist, Elementary Resource Teacher, Cooper Mountain Elementary School, Beaverton School District, Oregon

Lula Beatrice Harris, Pre-School Teacher, Marvin Avenue Children's Center, Los Angeles

Carol J. Knight, Kindergarten Teacher, Bushland School, Texas

Denise Madison, First Grade Teacher, Tanglewood Elementary School, Derby, Kansas

Ellen Marie Nally, Kindergarten Teacher, Tower Hill Early Childhood Center, Randolph, Massachusetts

Jeanne Stenson Whitesell, Second Grade Teacher, Gibbs International Studies Magnet School, Little Rock, Arkansas

**NEA
EARLY CHILDHOOD
EDUCATION SERIES**

Risk-Taking in Learning, K-3

Robert D. Young

A NATIONAL EDUCATION ASSOCIATION PUBLICATION

Printing History
   First Printing: September 1991

Note

The opinions expressed in this publication should not be construed as representing the policy or position of the National Education Association. Materials published by the NEA Professional Library are intended to be discussion documents for teachers who are concerned with specialized interests of the profession.

Library of Congress Cataloging-in-Publications Data

Young, Robert D. (Robert Douglas), 1957–
    Risk-taking in learning, K–3 / Robert D. Young.
       p.   cm. — (Early Childhood education series)
    Includes bibliographical references (p.).
    "Stock no. 0354–3–00"--.
    ISBN 0–8106–0354–3
    1. Education, Primary—United States—Activity programs.   2. Risk
-taking (Psychology)   3. Decision-making—Study and teaching
(Primary)—United States.   4. Problem solving—Study and teaching
(Primary)—United States.   I. Title.   II. Series: Early childhood
education series (Washington, D.C.
LB1537.Y64   1991
372'.01'9—dc20   91–3911
                                                    CIP

CONTENTS

Chapter 1

RISK-TAKING IN LEARNING

"May I have two volunteers?" I frequently asked this question of the children in my classroom. Each time almost every child was willing to volunteer. This question was also asked of the parents at the first parent meeting of the year. The results were always the same—never did a parent volunteer. Only after a few questions such as "What will I be expected to do?" and "What do you have in mind?" were answered would someone agree to volunteer. The parents actually wanted answers to such questions as "Can I be successful?" "Will I look foolish?" and "Will I embarrass myself?"

The children were eager to take a risk with no questions asked. The few parents who eventually agreed to volunteer needed guarantees that their self-esteem and integrity would not be threatened. The message of this activity is worrisome; somewhere between kindergarten and adulthood we lose that eagerness, that willingness to take a risk simply for the sake of learning something new. This loss creates adults who lead safe, low-risk lives and, in addition, contributes to the large number of adults who no longer actively pursue learning.

Shel Silverstein captured this dilemma in his poem "Alice":

She drank from a bottle called DRINK ME
And up she grew so tall,
She ate from a plate called TASTE ME
And down she shrank so small.
And so she changed, while other folks
Never tried nothin' at all. (p. 112)*

---

*"Alice" by Shel Silverstein, from *Where the Sidewalk Ends.* Copyright © 1974 by Evil Eye Music, Inc. Reprinted by permission of HarperCollins Publishers.

Children and adults who are unwilling to take risks usually will never try anything at all. Such an approach to life may be safe but it certainly is not either exciting or educational or fun.

RISK-TAKING BEHAVIOR

Risk-taking is the willingness to venture into the unknown. It is an eagerness to try something new and different without putting the primary focus on success or failure. Learning is the reward of taking risks.

Five levels of risk-taking behavior have been identified. It should be noted that these levels are not stages through which all individuals progress. Risk-taking behavior is not a developmental process in which an individual begins at the lowest level and proceeds through subsequent levels until the highest level is reached. The levels are not assigned an age-appropriate range; rather, the levels indicate the varying degrees of risk-taking behavior. It is possible that a young child will display the highest level of such behavior and continue in this way all through his/her life. However, it is more probable that the young child with a high level of risk-taking behavior gradually will regress to a lower level. A description of the five levels of risk-taking behavior follows.

The Uninhibited Risk-Taker

The uninhibited risk-taker displays the highest level of risk-taking behavior. This behavior is very common in young children, especially in the beginning stages of early childhood. The uninhibited risk-taker is the most eager and the most willing to experience new learning and truly views learning as its own reward. However, unless appropriate instructional programs are provided in an emotionally healthy environment, this behavior will not be sustained. Pressures to conform to school and peer norms and inappropriate educational practices that emphasize the product over the process contribute to the decrease in uninhibited risk-taking behavior.

The Analytical Risk-Taker

The second highest level of risk-taking behavior—analytical risk-taking—is common all through the early childhood years. The analytical risk-taker is eager and willing to experience new learning and sees this as its own reward, but is more calculating than the uninhibited risk-taker. The analytical risk-taker is more inclined to study the situation, analyzing important factors before engaging in the task. This is a very desirable level of risk-taking behavior, and in certain situations, is even more preferable than uninhibited risk-taking. Teachers should not feel that raising the analytical risk-taker to the level of the uninhibited risk-taker is necessary. Teachers should be aware, however, that the same things that destroy uninhibited risk-taking also will destroy analytical risk-taking.

The Cautious Risk-Taker

The third level of risk-taking behavior becomes more common in the later stages of the early childhood years due, in part, to the inappropriate practices and pressures mentioned above. This cautious behavior, found in very young children (less than three years of age), is more than anything else the result of parenting practices that stifle a child's interest and desire to explore the environment. The cautious risk-taker, though still interested and eager, is less willing to take risks in learning but is willing to watch others take the initial risks. This student overemphasizes the importance of success and failure and is also overly concerned with how others will perceive his/her performance. However, the cautious risk-taker secretly wants to be more uninhibited in learning. Because of this, the teacher can effectively guide this student to higher levels of risk-taking behavior with appropriate instructional practices.

The Inhibited Risk-Taker

The fourth level of risk-taking behavior is less common in the early childhood years but is too often a destination toward which many young children are headed. The inhibited risk-taker wants guarantees and assurances of what is expected and of what effect it will have. There is a great concern for doing everything "right." Often this student participates in a new learning experience only after much encouragement is given. Even then, entering the activity will be done with much hesitancy. Once an individual enters this level of risk-taking behavior, it is very difficult to achieve higher levels.

The Nonrisk-Taker

The lowest level of risk-taking behavior is not often seen in young children. At this level, no risk-taking behavior is evident. New learning experiences are avoided and often there is a "You can't make me" attitude toward these new learning experiences. Therefore, most valuable learning will not be attained. Only routine learning tasks that have preestablished steps and expectations will be attempted. Like the inhibited risk-taker, this student's learning behavior is very difficult to change.

RISK-TAKING AND AT-RISK CHILDREN

The term "at-risk" has been used to describe those children who are in danger of failing in school or of failing in life (20).* A significant number of at-risk children are minorities and children who use English as a second language. Although early risk-taking behaviors know no racial or language barriers,

---

*Numbers in parentheses appearing in the text refer to the References beginning on page 73.

these children tend to drop to lower levels more quickly and easily than other children. They often develop low fate-control, that is, little confidence that control over what happens in one's life rests with the individual (10). Children with low fate-control will not recognize the need for being a risk-taker in learning. Therefore, the lack of risks taken in learning causes a failure to learn to solve problems and make decisions, which will gravely affect their ability to learn and to apply learning to real-life situations.

The two most commonly used approaches for dealing with at-risk children are pull-out special education programs and grade retention. Both have proved to be ineffective for raising achievement of at-risk children to adequate levels (50). The most effective element for preventing future failure in school and in life, but one that is not always used to its full potential, is quality, developmentally appropriate early education that promotes risk-taking, problem solving, and decision making.

This early education should provide experiences to help children with low fate-control recognize and understand the influence they have on events and circumstances in their lives. Science experiments that control the variables, language activities that use the children's own language, and math problems that allow for the application of a variety of strategies all contribute to the development of high fate-control. This, in turn, will lead the at-risk child to a greater willingness to take risks in learning.

PROBLEM SOLVING AND DECISION MAKING

Risk-taking is a prerequisite to becoming an effective problem solver and decision maker. The 1980s saw educators giving increased attention to developing problem-solving and decision-making abilities. A primary goal of this kind of instruction is to have these abilities transfer to the child's world outside of school. Problem-solving and decision-making abilities, used throughout life, will make a person a more productive member of a society that is in need of many more productive citizens.

Both the National Council of Teachers of Mathematics (2) and the National Science Teachers Association (10) recommend that the educational system include problem solving and decision making as major goals of education. The changes in our society and in our world have created a special need for its citizens to be effective problem solvers and decision makers. Therefore, it is necessary to encourage children to take risks in their learning experiences. Children must be given opportunities to solve problems and make decisions in an environment that promotes risk-taking.

Engaging in problem-solving activities requires an organized process. Polya (44) recommended that problem solvers follow these four steps: (1) develop an understanding of the problem; (2) devise a plan; (3) implement the plan; and (4) evaluate the solution, modifying the plan if necessary. Developing certain skills would make the implementation of this process more effective (60). A basic knowledge base is needed for each specific problem to be solved. It is important to be able to identify, locate, obtain, analyze and evaluate needed information. The problem solver should possess independent and creative thinking skills as well as motivation and perseverance. Communication skills and the ability to work well with others also contribute to the successful implementation of the problem-solving process.

For children to become effective problem solvers, a positive view regarding failure must be developed. The risk-taker understands that success is not guaranteed; therefore, he/she recognizes failure as a learning experience. Thomas Edison explained over 10,000 unsuccessful attempts to construct a battery as "I have not failed, just discovered ten thousand ways that don't work" (10). The role of the teacher is crucial to the development of risk-taking abilities. It is the teacher who creates the classroom environment, atmosphere, and attitude. These are critical factors in determining whether children will take risks or "never try nothin' at all."

As a child acquires the skills and develops an understanding of the process of problem solving, the confidence level for risk-taking is greatly increased. With this confidence comes a positive view of failure. The risk-taker understands that mistakes will be made and that roadblocks and impasses will be encountered. Failure will occur; however, the risk-taker sees it not as a stopping point or final evaluation, but rather as a meaningful learning experience. Polya's (44) final step includes modifying the plan if necessary. Edison obviously made many modifications before his battery was a success.

THE TEACHER'S ROLE

The child's abilities to solve problems and make decisions and his/her willingness to take risks depend in large part on the classroom teacher. The teacher creates and establishes the classroom environment and it is this environment that either encourages or discourages risk-taking. Attitudes, acceptance of the child and the child's ideas, routines, and instructional procedures are some of the factors that contribute to the classroom environment. It is the role of the teacher to ensure that these and other factors are positive contributors to an environment that promotes risk-taking.

The teacher's attitude toward risk-taking is crucial. The teacher must be a risk-taker and model risk-taking behavior, including a positive view of failure. Unique and innovative ideas must be viewed as signs of life and growth (6). This applies both to the teacher's instructional practices as well as to the teacher's acceptance of the children and their ideas. It is of extreme importance that the teacher accept unconditionally all children for the unique and different individuals that they are. When this acceptance is given, risk-taking is much more likely to occur.

In an environment where risk-taking is encouraged, it is

important that the teacher provide a "safety net" (6) that offers developmentally appropriate materials and activities and prevents failures from shattering the child's attitude, initiative, or self-esteem. As previously mentioned, the risk-taker recognizes that failures will occur. At these times, the teacher should provide additional information or materials or possibly guide the child to discover how the process could be modified in order to make the next attempt more successful.

In doing this, the teacher helps the child to recognize the importance of the process. By lessening the significance placed on the product (a significance that often mistakenly convinces children that there is only one correct answer and those who don't know it are stupid), the child will be more willing to take risks. Just as all areas of the curriculum involve processes, risk-taking should be an integral part of the total school curriculum. Daily opportunities for risk-taking should be provided. These should be both "hands-on" and "minds-on" and allow children to experiment with and explore their world.

Although many educators believe that risk-taking has a significant influence on learning, many schools encourage an overly cautious approach to educating young children. This unfortunate caution is the result of the severely misplaced emphasis on academic achievement that ignores developmental levels, and on achievement tests that are not valid measures of children's learning or teacher's accountability (29). This emphasis has created overly structured and rigid instructional practices that are too difficult for children and consequently, are very damaging to their development. It has also created a system in which teachers and administrators are unwilling to take the risks necessary to change these practices. This system is part of a society where many states pay more money to garbage collectors than to teachers and spend more money to incarcerate a criminal than to educate a child; where the government spends billions of dollars to build military equipment, while schools are holding bake sales and carnivals to raise money to buy their materials and equipment; where the government tries to declare that ketchup is a vegetable in order to cut the costs of the free and reduced lunch program, and where instructional practices are determined by someone other than the trained professional who is in the classroom with the children on a daily basis.

The teacher's primary responsibility is not to appease this society with high test scores but rather to offer children a quality, developmentally appropriate education that promotes risk-taking. Children need to be risk-takers in order to develop the problem-solving and decision-making abilities necessary to make tomorrow's society better than today's. Children need teachers who are willing to take risks to provide this quality education. Teachers must be risk-takers for the benefit of today's children and tomorrow's society.

PROMOTING RISK-TAKING
IN YOUNG CHILDREN

In our field of early childhood education, we work with many children who are already skilled risk-takers. These are the uninhibited and the analytical risk-takers. They arrive in our classrooms with a natural curiosity and an eagerness to discover and learn about the world they live in. They thrive on the processes of exploration and experimentation. For these children, their risk-taking needs only regular maintenance.

Other children enter our classrooms less willing to take risks. They are the cautious, the inhibited, and the nonrisk-takers. Either the home environment or previous educational experiences possibly could be responsible for this attitude. Unfortunately, some teachers create an environment and present instruction in ways that discourage risk-taking. In these classrooms, even the uninhibited risk-takers eventually will lose their curiosity and eagerness to learn.

Other teachers take advantage of the numerous opportunities to build risk-taking abilities that exist in daily routines and in all areas of the curriculum. In these classrooms, the natural risk-takers will easily maintain their abilities and even solidify them as permanent parts of their learning styles. More inhibited children will gradually acquire the ability and willingness to take risks. They will be encouraged by observing the natural risk-takers having successful and enjoyable learning experiences. In this environment, their attempts will be allowed and encouraged, which will promote a greater willingness to take risks in the future.

Risk-taking behavior is found in an environment that is emotionally safe, where success is abundant, and failure is recognized as only a step in the process of attaining success. Therefore, the overall classroom environment, from the room arrangement to the attitudes found within, provides the foundation for promoting risk-taking in young children. All subjects should be presented in a manner that allows, accepts, and encourages children's risk-taking behavior. Three subjects in particular—math, science, and the language arts—lend themselves to this but too often are presented in a way that breaks the spirit of the risk-taker.

Several factors contribute to the inappropriate instructional practices in use today. Teachers are asked to teach much more material than ever before. Along with the traditional subject areas, teachers must also present lessons on nutrition, dental and health care, drug education, AIDS education, and fire safety as well as on various other topics. Even with these added responsibilities, expectations for achievement scores are at an all-time high. With so much material expected to be taught and so much expected to be gained, it is not surprising that the focus of language arts and math instruction is on the mass production of basic knowledge, on spelling, handwriting, and word-calling skills, and on computation for the purpose of raising achievement test scores. Science, if taught at all, is usually offered in isolated segments in alternating weeks.

It is difficult to cover all of the required material, but

steps can be taken to do this and in a developmentally appropriate way. One suggestion is to slow down and enjoy the process of children discovering knowledge and thinking. Another is to integrate subject content. Chapters 2–5 focus on the classroom environment, math, science, and the language arts and Chapter 6 is devoted to presenting these subject areas in an integrated fashion.

Chapters 2–6 begin with a description of the classrooms of Mrs. Offderhide and Ms. Jolley, who teach next door to each other in the early childhood wing of their elementary school. A discussion of risk-taking as it relates to the subject area in each chapter follows. Each chapter then concludes with a section on ideas and activities.

Chapter 2

THE CLASSROOM ENVIRONMENT

One morning as Mrs. Offderhide was collecting homework, Bruce failed to turn in his assignment. She implemented what she considered an effective motivational technique by telling the other students what had happened and asking them what grade they thought Bruce should receive. The children answered in unison, "Zero!"

In Ms. Jolley's classroom, homework and all other schoolwork actively involved the children in the learning process. They were encouraged to discover, to think, to explore, and to experiment at home as well as at school. As active participants, the students often initiated much of their own learning. Risk-taking was a standard component in this classroom environment. The children were allowed and encouraged to take risks and Ms. Jolley was a good role model of risk-taking behavior.

Each of these classrooms provides an environment that was created by the teacher. At the beginning of the school year, a group of children with a wide variety of abilities, interests, personalities, and learning styles entered each classroom. Mrs. Offderhide "whipped those kids into shape" and had them conforming to school rules and routines very early in the school year. The majority of these children gravitated to the expected norm, while those who did not were labeled either behavior problems, slow learners, or both. Ms. Jolley's classroom offered an environment that encouraged risk-taking. The children continued to grow, to develop, and to learn in their own individual ways. The wide variety of abilities, interests, personalities, and learning styles seen at the beginning of the school year was even more pronounced at the end of the year.

The classroom that encourages risk-taking embraces an attitude that communicates to each class member that he/she is a valuable person with important ideas. Each day the children and the teacher enter this room with great anticipation and expectations concerning the learning that is certain to happen. This environment offers an unconditional, positive regard to each individual (26). Acceptance here does not depend on meeting the expectations of others but rather on the simple fact that these young children are capable of learning in an environment that allows them to do so in unique and different ways. Conforming to preestablished norms is not demanded; rather, nonconforming behaviors are accepted, encouraged, and enjoyed.

A major feature of this classroom environment is that young students are given choices, their decisions are respected, and they learn to recognize the consequences of their decisions. Decision making is an ability that is acquired through practice and experience. Numerous opportunities exist for students to make decisions during the school day. It is important to utilize these opportunities so that young children can have the experience of making decisions and accepting the consequences of their decisions.

The materials provided also are important to an environment that promotes risk-taking. A variety of materials must be available, both in kind and in level of difficulty (e.g., easel painting with brushes of various sizes; hammers and saws of different sizes and weights for woodworking; collages made on construction paper, cardboard, wood, or tree bark; drums, rhythm sticks, harpsicords, xylophones, and other instruments; lined and unlined paper on which to write titles to drawings or student-authored books; and word-list picture books and books that challenge children's comprehension and analytical thinking). Some materials should be free-form to allow children to explore and experiment in their individual ways (e.g., clay used without cookie cutters or rolling pins; a variety of music for creative dance; discarded clothing for dramatic play; chalk, crayons, felt pens, ink pens, and calligraphy pens, and pencils for drawing on paper, sidewalks, wood, chalkboards, and even walls; finger painting with shaving cream with food coloring added or with different flavors of pudding). This will better meet the wide range of ability levels and interests of the children.

The classroom environment that encourages risk-taking will develop good decision makers and effective problem solvers. When these abilities are established early, they will lay the foundation for a lifetime of learning.

IDEAS AND ACTIVITIES

The Beginning of the School Day

Greetings

Greet all children at the door as they arrive. Offer a personalized comment to each child: "Is that a new dress?" "You can finish the painting you were working on yesterday right now if you'd like." If greeting each child at the door is impractical, be sure to speak to each one on entering the classroom.

Begin Learning

Once children arrive and are settled (coats, lunches, and other materials are in place), learning should begin. In many early childhood classrooms, children arrive at different times over a period of several minutes. DON'T MAKE THE EARLY ONES WAIT OR SIT AND WATCH TV!!! Get them involved in some learning activity such as the following:

- Learning centers: free choice or teacher-assigned,

- Sustained silent reading (with less emphasis on the silent because morning is a good time for new conversations),

- Journal writing (see Chapter 6),

21

- Music playing as children arrive (optional),

- Instructional games placed on tables,

- Fun group games being played so that children can join in as they arrive (e.g., Simon Says, I Spy, Mirror-Mirror).

Opening

The first large-group time is a good time for (1)sharing ideas and experiences, (2) discussing upcoming events, and (3) assigning jobs and responsibilities.

Sharing time: Avoid allowing this time to become boring for other children. Set up guidelines such as scheduling four students to share each day and having a question–answer time for the listeners to ask questions of the child who shared. *Discussing upcoming events:* Each morning, give the day's schedule to the children and mention any special events that will be forthcoming in the near future.

Assigning jobs and responsibilities: This opening group time is used for deciding who the helpers will be for the day. Usually, the teacher assigns a child to a particular job, but children can be allowed to choose their own jobs. This can be done in a fair way by charting who chooses when, and in what order. Children are eager to help in doing "real work" and teachers should take advantage of this to help them experience the pleasures of doing meaningful work (26). Possible jobs might include:

Line leaders,
Door holders,
Table washers,
Center inspectors,
Sleeper wakers, and
Message runners.

The Instructional Day

Special considerations should be made when planning instruction for the risk-taking environment (9, 43, 55).

Affective Development

The following suggestions will encourage affective development in the classroom.

1. Provide a psychologically safe environment that offers unconditional acceptance to each child. One activity that will help to produce this environment is called an "Encounter." One child is nominated by another. Any child can then say what he/she likes about the nominated child or tell something special that this child has done.
2. The children's interests and ideas should direct learning and influence planning and instruction.
3. Offer many real choices to children, encourage them to make decisions, and honor the decisions they make.
4. Allow plenty of time for students to fully experience their thinking, working, and playing.

Cognitive Development

The following suggestions will encourage cognitive development in the classroom.

1. Place the greater emphasis on the process, not the product.
2. Help children to discover patterns.
   a. Clothes have patterns.
   b. Create number patterns. Fill in the blanks:
   2, 4, 6,   , 8
   1, 2, 4, 8,   , 32,   , 128

c. Use colored cubes or shapes to build patterns such as:

AB, AAB, ABBA, ABC, etc.

d. Challenge children to find words that have interesting patterns (e.g., Mississippi, Alabama, level).

3. Use more open-ended questions (those that accept several answers). Reduce the number of closed questions used (those that require one correct answer). Examples:

a. Closed: "What will happen when I put this salt in the water?"

Open: "What do you think I am going to do with this material?"

Open: "What kind of experiments could we conduct with salt and water"?

b. When reading *Where the Wild Things Are* by Maurice Sendak (Harper and Row, 1963), go beyond questions such as, "What happened to Max's room?" and ask:

"What would the place where the wild things are be like if Max had stayed?" or ". . . had never come?"

"What was it like before Max came?"

"What would have happened if Max's boat had taken him to where the wild things are?"

c. When dealing with a problem that affects everyone in the class, such as one child's continuous temper tantrums, use open-ended questions with the other children:

"How do these tantrums disturb us?"

"What do you think causes these tantrums?"

"What can we do to help stop the tantrums?"

4. Promote higher level cognitive processes such as application, analysis, synthesis, and evaluation.

a. Apply information to real-life situations.
b. Break down objects or ideas into smaller parts and see how the parts relate and are organized.
c. Rearrange these analyzed parts into a new whole to gain a new perspective or understanding.
d. Use evidence, established criteria, and existing knowledge to make judgments.

(See Chapter 5 for more on cognitive processes.)

5. Develop observation, classification, and prediction skills.
   a. Group objects by one attribute, then by two attributes,by three, and so on.
   b. Group objects by purpose or function.
      Attach. "Why?" to the end of closed questions when appropriate.
   d. Make predicting and hypothesizing a regular part of learning activities in all subject areas.
6. Enhance creativity.
   a. Use a lot of dramatic play.
   b. Ask "What if . . .?" questions.
   c. Use free-form materials.
   d. Interfere as little as possible.
   e. Avoid providing models for children to copy.
7. Encourage children to solve real-life problems.
   a. Fishing for real-life problems (C. Newton, personal communication, June 1, 1990). Use a fishing pole with a magnet attached to the line and paper fish with gem clips for mouths. Have an open-ended problem situation written on the side; then have children catch a fish, share the situation, and offer a solution to the problem. Example problems:
      • Walking home from school, a stranger offers

you a ride.
- Another child offers you candy that looks like some kind of vitamin or pill.
- You are playing in your yard and your ball rolls across the street.
- Your parents are not at home and an adult you do not know comes to the door.
- You see a child take another child's lunch money.

   b. Role playing. Have children assume roles and act out a given real-life situation.

8. Encourage children to use a variety of strategies for solving problems. For example, have each child pick something he/she would like to learn to do. Each child can then study this skill and determine which materials and strategies will be needed to learn this skill. Practice schedules can be established and progress can be evaluated on a regular basis. (See Chapter 3 for more on problem-solving strategies).

9. Special occasions.

   a. Birthday books (B. Dorfman, personal communication, September 15, 1987). Each child draws a picture of what he/she would like to give the birthday child. A description of the picture gift is written underneath the picture by either the teacher or the child. All pictures are bound together to make a birthday book for the birthday child.

   b. Field trips. Involve the children in the planning of field trips. They can take part in the decision making regarding—
- Where to go (when appropriate).
- What to take.
- How to get there (types of transportation; using maps to chart the course).

- What is to be learned.
- How to use the experience for future learning.
- Expected behaviors.

The End of the School Day

The most common response to a parent's question of "What did you do in school today?" is "Nothing." To avoid this response and to help children practice and experience reflexive thinking and evaluation, conclude the school day with a wrap-up discussion asking (7):

- How was your day?
- What did you do?
- What did you learn?
- Did you enjoy your day?
- Why was it fun/not fun?
- With whom did you play/work?
- What plans do you have for your school day tomorrow?

Chapter 3

MATHEMATICS

After completing their daily math worksheets, the children checked their answers in a large-group activity led by the teacher. Mrs. Offderhide called on Emily to answer the problem 5 + 2. Emily was unsure of the answer she had written and began to count on her fingers. "Big girls don't count on their fingers," scolded Mrs. Offderhide. Emily then reluctantly answered "six." The teacher told her that she was wrong and asked the other children to help her. The children sang "5 + 2 is 7, 5 + 2 is 7" to the tune of that traditional playground taunt "nyah nyah-nyah nyah-nyah nyah."

Ms. Jolley's class was working with a variety of manipulatives during their math time. She was very impressed with Robert's construction of sets of seven and calculation of the total number of various combinations of sets. Miss Jolley asked Robert to demonstrate his technique to the other children. He explained, "Sets of seven are easy. They're like touchdowns. If you score one touchdown it's seven points. Two touchdowns are 14 points, three are 21 points, four are 28, and it keeps going just like that."

The techniques described above are representative of two beliefs concerning math instruction. Baroody (5) labeled these the Absorption Theory and the Cognitive Theory.

The Absorption Theory views math as a collection of facts and skills. The accumulation of these facts and skills is done through rote memorization. This stresses the belief that math requires perfection. This unreasonable belief of perfection convinces children that smart kids always give the correct answer without hesitation. Those who cannot do this are stupid. Children develop anxiety about math that leads them to invent ways to hide their wrongfully perceived stupidity. This approach eliminates children's willingness to take risks when learning math. It will also inhibit risk-taking behavior in other learning situations.

The Cognitive Theory understands that "how" math is taught is just as important as "what" is taught. The instructional emphasis is on the process rather than on the product. Short cuts and informal procedures used by children are allowed and encouraged. Learning activities focus on finding and using relationships such as "sevens are touchdowns." This allows children to utilize their strengths to build insights and understandings that develop genuine mathematical knowledge. Children not only learn the math procedures but also when and how to apply the appropriate procedures to a given problem.

Instruction based on the principles of the Cognitive Theory presents math as a problem-solving discipline in which children are encouraged to be risk-takers. Children should learn a variety of strategies for solving problems such as the following (30):

1. Look for patterns.
2. Draw a diagram.
3. Make a model.
4. Construct a table.
5. Guess and check.
6. Account for all possibilities.
7. Act it out.
8. Write a math sentence.
9. Break the problem into smaller parts.
10. Restate the problem.
11. Identify given and wanted information.
12. Change your point of view. (p. 115)

Several measures should be taken to ensure the effective instruction of problem solving (31). There should be an atmosphere of success. A good supply of problems should be provided that will challenge the children to study the problems analytically. Students should be encouraged to utilize several strategies. The teacher should raise creative, constructive questions during problem-solving activities and should provide a good model for children to follow. When these measures are present in the classroom, children will become accomplished risk-takers.

IDEAS AND ACTIVITIES

A child is more willing to take risks if a solid foundation of understanding is acquired. Developing an understanding of specific concepts (59) will provide this important foundation of mathematical thinking that will encourage risk-taking behavior.

Observing

Children should use all five senses when observing—

- A flower or vegetable garden,
- Food,
- Toys,
- "Feely" boxes or bags,
- Sounds,
- Smells

Sample Activity:

Collect various smells to be placed in paper cups (cottonballs can be saturated with lemon juice, grape juice, vinegar, perfume, after shave lotion, and so on). There should be two cups containing each smell. Give each child a cup. Have the children find their matches.

Classifying

Further challenge observation skills by having children group objects based on similarities. It should be understood that in the early stages of classification development, children may possibly begin classifying with one trait and then switch to another. The teacher should accept this behavior.

The early childhood classroom is filled with materials that can be classified. These include—

- Children (by height, eye color, favorite book, etc.),
- Furniture,
- Books,
- Blocks,
- Clothing,
- Manipulatives,
- Shells,
- Rocks,
- Crackers of different shape and size, and
- Cereal of different shape and size.

Steps to follow when classifying (25):

1. Children predict which object will appear most often
2. Classify the objects
3. Discuss characteristics of the groups
4. Count the number in each group
5. Graph the results
6. Compare predictions to the results.

Have several students apply their classifying skills to organizing something in the classroom environment such as the block area, the reading area, or the writing area. The children should decide on the criteria for classification (e.g., blocks by shape; books by kind). When the organization has been completed, the classification system should be explained to all of the other class members (L. Keckley, personal communication, October 5, 1990).

Comparing and Contrasting

Children can compare and contrast (look for similarities and for differences) the same materials that have been used for classification. Big–small, more–less, and other such concepts can be developed when comparing and contrasting.

Sample Activities:

1. Send children on a hunt for objects found outdoors such as leaves, rocks, shells, small sticks, and so on.. The class can be divided into groups with each group assigned an object to collect. For example, one group would look only for rocks. Back in the classroom, each group displays their objects on a table. Next, each group sorts its collection, comparing and contrasting objects in the same group. Children can label the objects that have been sorted (big rocks, smooth rocks, bumpy rocks, broken rocks).

2. Use a large number of objects that represent three or four varieties of the same characteristic (the set could have objects that are three or four different shapes or three or four different colors). The teacher places one object on the table. The first child places another object on the table that is different from the first object. The second child places an object on the table that is different from the one placed by the first child. The process continues until all objects are placed in a row on the table (58).

3. Use a large number of objects that represent three or four different varieties of two different characteristics (the set could have various shapes of various colors). The process is similar to the one mentioned above except that the next object placed on the table must have one characteristic that is the same and one that is different from the previous object (a red circle or

a green square could be placed next to a red square).

4. Divide the children into groups of five or six. Have each child remove one shoe and place it in a pile with the other shoes. One child then groups the shoes based on one property. Other children try to guess which property is being used for the grouping.

Seriating

Children use their abilities to observe, classify, compare and contrast in order to arrange objects in a series. Items can be placed in order according to—

- Short to tall,
- Light to heavy,
- Smooth to rough,
- Soft to hard,
- Small to large.

This concept can be developed by adapting the activities for comparing and contrasting to seriating.

Sample Activity:

Put different amounts of water into several bottles. Tap each bottle with a spoon or blow over the opening. Arrange the bottles in order from the lowest to the highest sound. This can also be done with bells of different size.

Patterning

Children can make—

Movement patterns by using different movements (bending, hopping, tiptoeing) in a specific sequence.

Sound patterns by using rhythm instruments.

Visual patterns with blocks, fabrics, colors, paint,

yarn, popped and unpopped popcorn, etc.

They can look for patterns in—

Clothes
Poetry
Songs
Buildings and houses
Nature (snowflakes, leaves, flowers).

See Chapter 2 for more ideas on patterning.

Graphing

All materials previously discussed can be charted on a graph. Graphing develops concepts such as one-to-one correspondence, one-to-many correspondence, more, less, equal, same, and different.

Almost anything can be graphed including:

- Birthdays by month,
- Weather (days of sunshine, clouds, rain, etc.),
- Number of teeth lost,
- Eye color,
- Hair color, and
- Shoe color.

Sample Graph (58):

For graphing that reflects characteristics of children, make a large graph and use a photograph of each child to represent the individual on the graph. When graphing eye color, the photographs of the children with a particular eye color can be placed in the designated row.

Measuring

Have children measure items using objects other than rulers, yardsticks, scales, or other standard measuring devices. Challenge children to discover new ways of measuring things. For example, children can determine—

1. How many pencils are needed to fill a box
2. How many children wide the room is
3. How many crayons long a desk is
4. How many children are needed to weigh as much as the teacher
5. How much more water (or beans, rice, paperclips) one glass holds than another
6. How many pennies (or paperclips) a pencil weighs.

Counting

Counting becomes meaningful when it is given a purpose that is important and of interest to children. Therefore, count to determine—

How many children like chocolate ice cream best (then compare to the numbers that like vanilla and strawberry best).

How many petals each flower has.

How many raisins really are in a bowl of raisin bran.

Give each child ten teddy graham bears. To the tune of "Brown Bear, Brown Bear" the teacher and the children should chant:

"First Grade, (or kindergarten)
First Grade,
What do you see?
We see ten bears looking at us."
(and they count:)

36

"1–2–3–4–5–6–7–8–9–10,
And we gobble one up."
(Each child eats one bear.)

The chant is repeated until all bears are eaten (S. H. Armstrong, personal communication, October 2, 1990).

Estimating

Estimating is an excellent activity to use for promoting risk-taking in learning. When the following questions are posed (41), either two or three choices can be given or no choices given at all, depending on the needs of the children.

"About how many children are in first grade at our school?"

"In Mrs. Smith's class, there are about how many children?"

"How many children are in this whole elementary school?"

"About how many children will be needed to lift the sandtable?"

"How many more drops of water can be put in this full glass of water?"

"How many pennies (paperclips, pencils, crayons) can you pick up with one hand? With two hands?"

"How many science books will be needed in a stack to be as tall as a stack of ten math books?"

"How many children will be absent all next week?"

The following activities challenge children to estimate (41):

1. Take the children to the library and ask each child to find two books, one that has two times the number of pages as the other. Children are not allowed to open the books while they look for their selections. Also, have children find two books that have the same number of pages, again without opening the books.

2. When you conduct the measuring activities mentioned

37

earlier, have the children estimate how many children long the room is after measuring how many children wide the room is.

Also when measuring, begin taking a measurement such as how many crayons long a desk is. After a portion of the desk has been measured, for example, when three or four crayons have been put in place, ask children to estimate how many crayons will be needed for the whole measure.

3. Fill three containers (more depending on students' ability level) with varying amounts of counters. Have the children arrange the containers in order from the one with the most to the one with the least. Then have the children count the contents of the container in the middle and estimate the number in the two remaining containers.

4. Place a large number of objects in a jar. Have the children estimate how many objects are in the jar, write their estimates on slips of paper, and place them in a ballot box. At the end of the day (week or month), the contents are counted and estimates are evaluated. A second jar containing ten objects and labeled "This is ten" can be used to help formulate estimates. Contents can be marbles, pencils, crayons, erasers, or any other common object. They can also be seasonal, for example, popcorn kernels for September (to be popped after counting), black and orange jelly beans for October, Christmas tree ornaments for December, paper or candied hearts for February, flower seeds for April (E. B. Harris, personal communication, June 1, 1990).

Analytical Thinking

A child's ability to use reason, logic, and analytical thinking will greatly influence risk-taking behavior. The following are activities to promote these abilities.

The Detective Game (R. Reed, personal communication, June 3, 1981). Two children chosen to be the detectives leave the room. Two other children are selected to be the suspects for the crime. One suspect always lies, the other always tells the truth. One is guilty, the other is innocent. These roles should be assigned while the detectives are out of the room. When the detectives return, they are allowed to ask two questions (two total, not a piece) to determine who is guilty beyond any shadow of a doubt. Hint: the first question should be rhetorical.

The Advanced Detective Game (R. Reed, personal communication, June 3, 1981). The two detectives leave the room. There are three suspects for this crime. One suspect always lies, one always tells the truth, and one sometimes lies and sometimes tells the truth. One is guilty, the other two are innocent. The detectives now have four questions to ask to determine who is guilty beyond any shadow of a doubt.

Wheels (33). Our school's playground equipment includes 15 tricycles and two-wheeled scooters. The total number of wheels on the tricycles and scooters is 38. How many tricycles and how many scooters does our school have?

What's My Shape? (42) Place several shapes in a grab bag. One child reaches into the bag, chooses a shape, and without removing it from the bag, describes it to the rest of the children. Depending on the ability level, the child could choose a shape and guess what it is or the teacher could instruct the child to find a specific shape in the bag.

Guess the Number (22). This activity can be done in either large group, small group, or pairs. It could be done with one person thinking of a number and giving clues, or cards with the number and the clues written on it can be used. The children have to try to determine the number after each clue is given. Only one guess per clue. Example clues are—

> It is an even number.
> It is less than 25.
> It is between 20 and 40.
> The sum of its digits is eight.
> Both digits are odd numbers.
> Neither number begins with an "f."

One digit number is two times the other.
Both digits are the same number.

Cooking (15). Tell the children that one cook can cook a dozen hamburgers in ten minutes while another cook takes two hours (or say 120 minutes) to cook a dozen hamburgers. Have children discuss why it takes the second cook so much longer to cook the hamburgers.

Up or Down (15)? Take ten coins and form a triangle with four on the bottom row, three in the next row, then two, then one on top. Ask a child to move any three coins and make the triangle point down instead of up. For an easier version, use six coins in three rows and ask a child to move any two coins.

Lining Up (15). Give one card to each child. On the cards are written instructions for the order of the line. Have the children arrange themselves in the proper order. This can be done with either the whole class or with a small group. The number and the difficulty of the clues will depend on the children's ability level. Example clues are—

You are behind Amy and in front of David.
You are third from the front.
You are last.
You are two places behind Derek.
Erin is behind you.
You are between the first person and Kim.

This can also be done on a walking number line and example clues would be—

You are two numbers less than seven.
You are one number behind Ricky.
Three plus four equals your number.

Handshakes (15). Have the children act this out after making predictions. Five children meet at a table for lunch. Each person shakes hands with everyone else. How many handshakes will take place?

Income (15). Ask children which classroom job they would prefer, and why, if you began paying for the work.

1. Line Leader—$25 a month
2. Door Holder—$8 a week
3. Table Washer—$1 a day
4. Center Inspector—$50 for the whole year.

Long Life (15). Have children determine how many months (weeks, days, hours, minutes, or seconds) they have been alive. This is a good activity for using calculators.

Heads or Tails. Give each child a coin. Make a graph that shows the number of heads and tails for each flip for five to ten flips. Before each flip, children can predict how their coin will land and whether there will be more heads or tails.

Toothpick Triangles (34). Ask the children to use six toothpicks to make four congruent equilateral triangles. Hint: The Egyptians did this with their pyramids.

One-Lane Bridge (34). Ask how can two cars traveling in opposite directions on the same road cross a one-lane bridge without having an accident?

Paperclip Designs. Use one paperclip and two pencils to produce creative and abstract designs. Place one pencil inside the paperclip, holding the pencil in place on a piece of paper. Place the second pencil at another point inside the paperclip. Move this pencil in a circular motion around the first pencil. Change the positions of the pencils to add more to the design.

Chapter 4

SCIENCE

It is 1:35 on Thursday afternoon and Mrs. Offderhide is teaching science because it is 1:35 on Thursday afternoon. This is the scheduled beginning time for one of the two weekly 45-minute periods for science. This lesson, like most science lessons, involves having the children read from the textbook and then Mrs. Offderhide asks questions from the teacher's manual. Adam stated, "This is boring." He was immediately placed in isolation (probably for telling the truth).

In Ms. Jolley's classroom, integrating science into the reading program is one of a variety of methods used to teach science. This approach involves much individual as well as small-group work. A guided discovery science experiment is a regular part of the reading lesson. For this experiment, students, working independently, would first record their hypotheses in their science journals. Next, they would follow the written instructions for conducting the experiment. Upon completion of the experiment, they would make a written evaluation of the experience in their science journals.

Mrs. Offderhide's classroom is an example of an authoritarian approach. The authoritarian teacher demands obedience and discourages freedom to think and to question. This approach is antiscientific (10). By not allowing children to question any answers, skepticism—a necessary attitude for scientific inquiry —fails to develop in young children.

Ms. Jolley views a lecture format as inappropriate for use with young children. Science is perfectly suited for "hands-on" and "minds-on" activities. Her science program offers a variety of instructional methods. This program involves children with science in the following ways (10):

1. Listening-Speaking: auditory learning, students learn by hearing;
2. Reading-Writing: visual learning, students learn by seeing;
3. Watching-Doing: kinesthetic learning, students learn by doing. (p. 89)

Young children's fascination with their world should be the foundation for the early childhood science program. They naturally seek knowledge and understanding. Their curiosity makes them natural learners and natural risk takers. A science program that builds a healthy skepticism, challenges children to continue to explore their world, and teaches them to have a positive attitude about failure will establish a lifelong desire for knowledge and a willingness to take the risks to acquire it.

IDEAS AND ACTIVITIES

Dewey (14) believed that a child's thinking processes were very similar to those of a scientist. Just as we would never attempt to restrict the thinking of a scientist, we should never restrict the thinking of a child.

Flying

Give each child a piece of paper. Challenge the children to find the way to make the paper travel through air the farthest possible distance.

Display pictures of various types of kites. Ask children to collect the materials needed to build a kite. Allow children to build kites, to test the kites' abilities to fly, and to continue to make needed adjustments.

Have children experiment with building parachutes. Allow them to decide what materials to use. Challenge the children to:

- Build the slowest parachute.
- Build a parachute that can carry an egg without

breaking it.
- Land the parachute in a designated area.

Attach self-addressed, stamped postcards to helium-filled balloons with the activity explained on the card, requesting the finder to write where the card was found and return it through the mail. Release the balloons. Display a map of the United States and stick pins with children's names at the landing points of each balloon.

Light

Provide children with mirrors and flashlights. Pair a child with a mirror with a child with a flashlight. Allow them to discover how the mirror can receive and send the beam of light. Children may attempt to send one beam of light from mirror to mirror (38).

Introduce children to sundials. Ask them to create their own sundials. Ask them to mark the different times on the sundial and write instructions for its use. Allow the children to decide on all of the materials to be used.

To plot the earth's orbit around the sun, have the children measure the length of the shadow of a pole on the playground at a set time on the first day of each month throughout the school year. The children can predict the length and location of the shadow each month and discuss how and why the shadow changes (35).

Water and Ice (36)

Fill a container to the brim with ice cubes and water. Have children make hypotheses concerning what will happen when the ice floating above the water melts.

Place a plastic soft drink bottle filled with water and closed with a screwtop cap in a freezer. Have children offer hypotheses about what will happen. Additional plastic bottles can be used, for example, one, half-full of water; one, full of water but uncapped. Caution: never do this with glass bottles.

Give each child in the class an ice cube and challenge them to keep the cube as large as possible. Ice cubes can be compared at the end of a set time period (30, 45, or 60 minutes).

Give each child an ice cube and a paper towel. All ice cubes should be of equal size. Determine who can melt the ice cube the fastest. No swallowing allowed.

To determine children's preferred temperature of a cold drink, provide several containers of ice water at various temperatures. Have each child taste test to determine the preferred temperature. This can be done with hot chocolate, also.

For homework, challenge children to create an ice cube with a very strange shape—possibly, even a round ice cube.

Clay Boats. (3). Give each child a ball of clay. Ask them to make it float in a tub of water.

Evaporation. Fill several same-size glasses with the same amount of water. Place the glasses in different parts of the room. Have the children record the amount of evaporation every one to two days. Another activity to demonstrate is to use a sponge and a bucket of water, and wet down various areas or items inside and outside the classroom, such as the chalkboard, the window, the carpet, a desktop, the asphalt play area, sand, or a grassy area. Children should then be asked to predict the drying or evaporation time. Predictions and results should be recorded, compared, and analyzed (E. Beard, personal communication, October 4, 1990).

Insulation. Challenge children to determine the best materials to use for insulation. Pieces of ice can be wrapped in aluminum foil, tissues, plastic wrap, different kinds of paper, cotton, wool, sand, and so on, in order to determine which material is the best insulator (E. Beard, personal communication, October 4, 1990).

Changing Temperatures. Fill one bowl with ice and one with hot water. Place a thermometer in each bowl. Record the temperatures when each reaches its extreme, then record the temperatures at set time intervals until each reaches room temperature.

Place a ping pong ball in a tall, thin glass (or clear plastic) cylinder. The cylinder should be tall enough and thin enough so that a child's hand cannot fit down inside. Challenge the children to think of as many ways as they can to remove the ball from the cylinder. Any material can be used. Strategies should be recorded, tested, and evaluated. Children will use string, tape, and bubble gum, but water works best.

Drying the Chalkboard. Assign the children to small cooperative groups. Present them with the task of drying a wet chalkboard (sponges can be used to wet the chalkboard). The groups should devise three strategies, testing each to determine the best method for drying the board. Hair dryers, bellows, bath towels, paper towels, fans, and other methods might be used (S. Bratton, personal communication, October 15, 1990).

The Environment

Use commercials that make claims such as the cereal that meets the daily requirements of all essential vitamins and have children investigate the truth of the claims. With this cereal, students could compare the list of vitamins found on the box to the requirements set by the FDA (4).

To demonstrate the consequences of an acid environment (37):

Prepare an acid environment by placing vinegar-soaked paper towels around the classroom 10 minutes before the children arrive. Ask the children to contrast the acid environment with their normal environment.

Place an egg in a covered jar of vinegar. Ask children to predict what will happen. Have children observe and analyze the results.

Stand a penny on end in a small piece of clay. Place it into

47

a covered jar of vinegar-soaked paper towels. Children can predict what will happen, then observe, and analyze the results.

Put granite in an acid solution. While children observe the reaction, stress how acid rain combined with rocks and soil destroys life in rivers and lakes.

To stress the need for recycling:

Have children collect items for recycling (soft drink cans, old newspapers, etc.). Take a field trip to a recycling center.

Collect many things from the classroom that are usually thrown away (broken pencils or those too short to write with, edges torn off computer paper, empty paint containers, scraps of construction paper, the last tiny bits of yarn). Pass these out to the children and challenge them to find a use for each item.

To demonstrate the unpleasantness of pollution, don't throw away anything for a week. Used materials and those no longer needed should be discarded at random, cluttering the floor, tables, and shelves. When the litter reaches the point of being very unpleasant, discuss the consequences of pollution and the steps that can be taken to ease the burden of pollution.

Find a place where there is a lot of litter. Take a field trip to this place to collect the litter. Each child should have a bag in which to collect litter. Caution children not to pick up broken glass. "Before" and "After" pictures can be drawn on location or after returning to the classroom.

World Globes (K. Wallace, personal communication, September 19, 1990). Blow up a balloon to the desired size. Cut newspapers into strips and dip them into a solution of one part water and one part glue. Lightly run fingers down the strips to remove the excess solution. Cover the balloon with one thin layer of strips. Let dry overnight. Apply a second layer of strips the next day. Let dry overnight. Paint the whole globe blue for the oceans. Then paint the continents or make continents using construction paper and glue these onto the globe.

Decomposition (L. Keckley, personal communication, October 5, 1990). After lunch one day, collect the leftover food, eating utensils, and paper. Place half of everything collected in a mesh bag and bury it outside, approximately one and a half feet below the surface. Of the remaining items, place utensils into one plastic zip-lock bag, paper products into another, and each individual food item into separate bags. In one bag, place a sample of each (a fork, some paper, a little milk, some meat, and vegetables). Place the plastic bags where they can be observed on a daily basis. Ask children to predict what will happen in each bag. Daily observations should be made and recorded for the contents of the plastic bags. The mesh bag should be uncovered once a week and its contents studied, compared, and contrasted with the contents of the plastic bags.

Challenge children to determine the relationship between space and weight. Allow them to experiment with materials of various sizes to determine the effect of size on weight. Materials can include lead, styrofoam, wood, plastic, liquid, etc. (E. Beard, personal communication, October 4, 1990).

Pendulums (39)

To make a pendulum requires a piece of string, a weight, and, in some cases, a frame to hold the pendulum. The weight can be a washer, a piece of wood, a ball, or many other things. Allow children to find their own weights. Pendulum activities can teach terms such as frequency and period (the time it takes the weight to go back and forth one time).

Have children experiment with shortening and lengthening the string of their pendulums and discover how this affects the frequency and period. Children can count the number of periods of pendulums of varying lengths in a set time frame (10 seconds).

Compare the period of the same pendulum as it swings in a straight line and then in a circle.

Create pendulum games with golf tees. Arrange the tees in various designs and shapes. Swing the pendulum in ways that knock down the tees and in ways to avoid knocking down the tees. Allow children to create their own games.

Place two pendulums of the same length and weight side by side. Swing them so that they swing together, swing in opposite directions, and swing in a crisscross pattern without colliding.

Use a paint brush as a weight. The tip of the brush should touch the paper that is placed beneath the pendulum. Dip the brush in paint and create pendulum paintings.

Dinosaurs (57)

Cut dinosaur footprints from oaktag. Footprints can be sorted by size and shape. Children can then match the footprints to the picture of the dinosaur that made each footprint.

Make fossils from clay, leaves, and seashells. These can be buried in a large sandbox and the children can conduct a fossil dig.

Have children draw, write, or tell about how and why dinosaurs became extinct.

Have children imagine that dinosaurs are still living today. Ask them to draw, write, or tell how this would change their lives. Ask how people would treat the dinosaurs and what we could do to prevent them from becoming extinct.

Ask the children to pretend to be dinosaurs. Have them write stories about their behavior, what they like to eat, what they do during the day, their fears, their ideas, and so forth.

Seasons (17)

Fall

Have children predict which trees will lose their leaves first and which will lose theirs last. Predict how many leaves a tree will lose in one day. Collect the leaves under that tree each day to determine how many actually fell.

Display weathervanes to the children. Challenge them to use any materials to create their own working weathervane.

Winter

After a good snowfall, have children find where the snow is the deepest and where it is the shallowest. They may use rulers or sticks to measure the depth of the snowfall.

Have children find animal tracks in the snow and make a sketch of the tracks. They can draw pictures of the animals they think made each track. Further study can be done using textbooks and encyclopedias to determine the animal that made each track.

Spring

After a rain, have children predict where they might find puddles. Upon locating a puddle, have the children measure its width and depth. They can then predict how long a puddle will last before it disappears.

Have children collect various objects of different weights. Place the objects in a straight line outside. Children can predict which ones will be moved by the wind, which ones will move the most, and which ones will move the least. Predictions should be compared to the actual results.

Summer

Place several types of food of various sizes near an anthill. Have children predict which foods the ants either will like or not like. Observe and record the results. Compare the results to predictions.

Prior to a field trip to a lake or a wooded area, discuss which animals may be seen and where they might be found. Explore the area with the children to discover the answers.

Plants and Animals

Category Cards (11). One child draws a card on which a category is written. This child names examples of this category. The other children guess the name of the category. The following are sample categories:

- Dinosaurs
- Birds
- Farm animals
- Sea animals
- Wild animals

- Types of weather
- Clouds
- Vegetables
- Fruits

Mystery Garden. Have children plant unknown vegetable seeds. As the plants grow, the children should use various resources to study the different parts such as the seeds, stem, and leaves to try to determine the identity of each vegetable.

Put a stalk of celery into water that has been mixed with food coloring. Over a period of several days, have children observe the celery leaves and the stalk.

Put a wet towel in each of two dishes. Place seeds on the towels and cover with another wet towel. Put one dish in a warm place and the other in a cool place. Have the children observe the seeds each day and record the growth progress.

Animal Habitats. Select a hole in the ground where you think an animal lives. Clear the immediate area of leaves, sticks, and rocks. Spread flour around the hole. Return the next day and study the tracks made in the flour. Try to determine which animal lives in the hole.

Bird Feathers. To determine whether birds get wet when it rains, collect various bird feathers. Put a drop of water on each one. Study what happens to the water on each feather.

Chapter 5

THE LANGUAGE ARTS

Friday morning after the low reading group had finished the round-robin reading lesson with Mrs. Offderhide, the entire class prepared for the weekly spelling test. Words were given and spelled (and misspelled), after which papers were exchanged for grading. Each child then wrote any misspelled word ten times on the board. Surprisingly, Bobby did not mind doing this since he had long ago mastered the technique of holding two pieces of chalk in one hand and writing the same word twice. He obviously had had plenty of practice time with misspelled words as well as with sentences such as "I will not talk in class."

Next door, Ms. Jolley was reading a Big Book to a small group of children. The story was familiar to the children and they often read along with the repetitive verses. In another part of the room, Victoria was sitting in a rocking chair reading to a group of friends a collection of poems she had written. Other children were scattered around the room. Some were sharing a book with a friend, others were reading independently, while some were writing in journals or producing student-authored books utilizing the invented spelling that Ms. Jolley encouraged them to use. By using invented spelling, they could write the words they wanted to use, not just the words they knew how to spell. Though everyone was intensely involved in some activity, the atmosphere in the room was very relaxed and comfortable.

Traditional early childhood practice has been to teach reading-readiness skills first. When these were mastered, then formal reading instruction began (19). Once children could read and spell, then handwriting (not to be confused with composition) was taught, but always separately from reading. The most common instructional method was the use of the workbook or ditto sheet that emphasized a specific skill or subskill.

This practice is still commonly used in many early childhood classrooms for several reasons (19). Publishing companies offer attractive and efficient paper–pencil materials that provide tangible, accountable measures of children's performance. Also, parents and society in general are demanding high achievement and are using achievement test scores as the primary measure of success. Even though the skills mastered from workbooks rarely transfer to meaningful reading and writing activities, they often resemble material found on achievement tests, thus giving the appearance of high achievement.

However, recent evidence indicates that this practice ignores how young children actually achieve literacy (21, 23, 24, 52, 54). Before children enter kindergarten they are developing as readers and writers. Reading and writing are interrelated processes that develop through activities in the child's natural world.

Emergent literacy is an active developmental process in which children construct knowledge about reading and writing (19). Children use print in all areas of learning. Therefore, an environment is provided that is rich in many forms of print such as quality literature, children's writing, experience charts, posters, and signs. Learning activities offer opportunities for social interaction as well as for individual work. The focus of emergent literacy is on the children. With this approach, children develop the knowledge and understanding they need to become effective communicators and quality readers and writers.

IDEAS AND ACTIVITIES

Oral Language

Use group discussions to promote oral language development.

Topics can include (46)—

1. Moral and ethical situations found within quality literature.
2. The characteristics of a good person; a bad person.
3. Current events that children are aware of and interested in such as elections, natural disasters, international conflicts, etc.

Invite a senior citizen with an unusual background to class to share memories and experiences. Allow children to question the visitor (46).

Ask the children to talk to their grandparents and/or other older relatives and family friends about the things they did and experienced (46).

Have children explain the meanings of old sayings such as—

- Wet behind the ears
- Only the tip of the iceberg
- You can't see the forest for the trees
- Faith moves mountains
- Don't cry over spilled milk
- One hand washes the other
- Keep your nose to the grindstone
- Let your conscience be your guide.

Have children finish partial old sayings such as—

- A bird in hand is worth . . .
- Where there's smoke, there's . . .
- A penny saved is . . .
- Two wrongs don't . . .
- A miss is as good as . . .
- Don't cry over . . .
- You scratch my back, I'll . . .
- Beauty is only . . .

Have children test the accuracy of old sayings and superstitions such as—

- Water seeks its own level
- Where there's smoke, there's fire
- Knock on wood
- Friday the thirteenth
- You can lead a horse to water but you can't make him drink
- A picture is worth a thousand words.

Have children explain how superstitions such as the following came to be—

- Knock on wood
- Friday the thirteenth
- Stepping on a crack
- A black cat crossing your path
- Never walk under a ladder.

Children enjoy playing games with words and they are fortunate that the English language provides a wealth of opportunities to make games with words. Children can have fun with synonyms, antonyms, and homonyms, with parts of speech and figures of speech, and with sound words and slang words (13). Children's literature is a good source to encourage and stimulate children in their play with words (see Bibliography for book list). After reading a book such as *What's a Frank Frank? Tasty Homograph Riddles* by Giulio Maestro (Clarion Books, 1984), children can be encouraged to create their own riddles to share with each other.

Storytelling

Storytelling is an excellent technique for promoting risk-taking, both for the teacher and the children. Storytelling

56

requires an uninhibited performer, which is the reason many adults shy away from this activity. But the teacher who enthusiastically presents storytelling provides a valuable and exciting learning experience for the children, while at the same time serving as a good role model for risk-taking behavior. Children will want to join in on the storytelling fun and become uninhibited storytellers themselves. Guidelines for storytelling follow (56):

1. The story you tell should be one that you enjoy and believe others will enjoy.
2. The length of the story should be appropriate for the listeners.
3. When you prepare your story, focus on the sequence, plot, and setting instead of simply memorizing the words.
4. Speak clearly and with effective pace, tone, and intonation.
5. Use body language to help tell the story and keep the listeners interested.
6. Relax.
7. Be unique.
8. Have fun.

Props often add to the interest and enjoyment of the story. One example of using a prop to help tell a story is shown in the paper-cutting story (40). This technique has the storyteller cutting an object out of a piece of folded construction paper while telling the story. The cutting adds excitement if the cutting steps relate to the story.

Objects that can be cut with a story include:

1. A pig for "The Three Little Pigs"
2. A ghost for Halloween stories
3. A butterfly for *The Very Hungry Caterpillar* by Eric Carle (Philomel Books, 1969)

4. A tortoise for "The Hare and the Tortoise"
5. A bear for "Goldilocks and the Three Bears."

Once children are familiar with the story they can take part in the cutting and even make up their own stories and objects to cut.

Dramatic Play

Dramatic play is an area of the early childhood environment that commonly provides an excellent setting for risk-taking behavior. This area also is very effective for promoting language development, both oral and written. In order to stimulate written language development, supply reading and writing materials that are common to the home, office, grocery store, post office, fire station, toy store, restaurant, and so on. Some of these materials are note pads, pencils, telephone directories, grocery items, mail (bring your junk mail from home), books, cookbooks, food coupons, stationery, and maps.

Allow children to make their own props to use in their dramatic play. Boxes of all sizes are great for this (32).

Children can make a roller movie of their favorite original stories (32).

Provide a wide assortment of puppets, purchased, teacher-made, and child-made, along with a puppet theater.

Writing

Make a bulletin board into a message board that is reserved for the written exchange of special news. Any class member, teacher or child, can leave a message on the board for someone. The person receiving the message removes it from the board, reads it, and responds in writing, leaving the response on the message board for the intended person (45).

Involve children in creating the newsletters sent to parents by (51)—

Allowing children to be illustrators: they can draw children in the class, a classroom pet, a field trip.

Allowing children to be reporters: they can interview each other, the teacher, the principal, or report on exciting classroom and school events.

Allowing children to be editors: they can arrange the layout of the newsletter, assign topics to reporters.

Illustrations can add to children's writing and also encourage and stimulate further writing. Allow children to use calligraphy pens and scraps of wallpaper, newspaper, construction paper, and fabrics for their illustrations (32). Studying the illustrations in books by Ezra Jack Keats could encourage children to use these materials. See, for example, *Dreams* (Macmillan, 1974), *Goggles* (Macmillan, 1969), *Hi Cat* (Macmillan, 1970).

Encourage children to make several illustrations to tell the story of their favorite Christmas carol (32).

Challenge children to study the illustrations of Margaret Wise Brown's *The Runaway Bunny* (Harper and Row, 1942) and *Goodnight Moon* (Harper and Row, 1947)to try to determine which book was written first.

Write vocabulary words in a tic-tac-toe grid. Have children work in pairs. To earn a square, a child must write a sentence that correctly uses the vocabulary word found in the square. When the word is used correctly, an "X" or "O" is placed in the square. The game continues like a tic-tac-toe game in this way (K. Wallace, personal communication, September 19, 1990).

Provide two or three examples of picture words. Challenge the children to create their own picture words. Examples:

```
stereo      (stereotype)

bana  na       (banana split)

T

O

U       (touchdown)

C

H
```

Make an "-ish" book for each season (C. H. Gilley, personal communication, October 2, 1990). An "-ish" statement should be written at the top of each page. For example, "Fall is red-ish," "Winter is cold-ish," "Spring is rain-ish," "Summer is fun-ish." On each page, the children should draw a picture or write a description of the "-ish" statement.

Poetry

The freedom of expression offered in poetry makes it an effective learning experience for promoting risk-taking behavior. Ideas for getting poetry started and keeping it going include the following (48):

Divide the chalkboard into several sections. Label each section according to the type of words desired (e.g., action words, funny words, feeling words). Ask the children to provide words for each category.

Encourage children to write haiku (three lines: first and third lines have five syllables, second line has seven) and cinquain (five lines: first line has one word giving the title, second line has two words describing the title, third line has three words expressing an action, fourth line has four words expressing a feeling, and the fifth line has one word that is a synonym for the title).

Allow children to illustrate their poems using a variety of materials.

Provide a variety of poetry books for children to enjoy (see Bibliography for list of children's poetry books). Also provide and encourage children to collect verses from greeting cards.

Make a PoeTree (27) in the classroom. The tree can be placed on a wall, hung like a mobile, or "planted" in a flower pot. Poems written and illustrated by children can be hung from the branches along with their favorite poems.

Create a group poem (1). The teacher or a child writes the first line of a poem on the board. The next child adds a second line to the poem. Another child writes the next line, and so on until a poem is written. This does not have to be done in a group setting. The poem can be left on a board for children to add to when a new line is created.

Critical Thinking

Bloom's *Taxonomy of Educational Objectives, Cognitive Domain* (8) can serve as a guide to applying critical thinking activities to children's literature. Examples of general discussion points for each level include:

Knowledge: Discuss the basic facts important to the story. Have children retell the story.

Comprehension: Ask children to make inferences and give explanations about specific situations in the story.

Application: Have children apply information or events found in the story to actual situations. Encourage children to investigate topics related to the story.

Analysis: Ideas can be broken down into simple parts and analyzed. Children can compare and contrast the behavior and development of the characters in the story.

Synthesis: The story's component ideas can be rearranged into a new whole, such as having children role play a new ending to the story.

Evaluation: Ask children to make value judgments and offer opinions based on external and internal evaluation.

The following example uses the questioning techniques based on Bloom's *Taxonomy* with Ezra Jack Keats's book *Apt. 3:* (Macmillan, 1971).

Knowledge: What did Sam hear? What kind of instrument made the music?

Comprehension: What was Sam trying to do when he went into the hall? Why do you think Ben tagged along? How did Sam feel about Betsy?

Application: Have you ever gone looking for something that both interested and scared you? Tell us about someone you know who is like the harmonica player.

Analysis: How did the feelings Sam experienced change throughout the story? What caused his feelings to change each time?

Synthesis: After experiencing all these feelings, how will it affect Sam's feelings tomorrow? How would Sam have reacted if the music had been coming from Betsy's apartment?

Evaluation: Was it okay for Sam to go searching for the music? What was the harmonica player's answer about the walk? Why did he give this answer?

Any selection of children's literature can be a tool for teaching critical thinking. The following procedure is suggested (53):

1. Select a book that is of interest to your children. Books with a repetitive plot and a small number of characters are preferable.

2. Read the story several times so that it is well understood by the children.

3. Discuss the characters, their actions and behaviors, the problems they encounter, and how the problems were resolved.

4. Have children assume the role of a character. Ask them to describe how they would respond in certain situations within the story. Pose alternative situations not found in the story and ask them how they would respond to these.

5. The children can create a play or puppet play based on the story but offering a different version.

Another approach to teaching critical thinking is to stimulate discussion about fact and opinion. This can be done by writing true, false, and opinion statements on cards and playing a game in pairs or small groups (11). One child can draw a card, read the statement, and state whether it is true, false, or opinion. The other child or children can agree or disagree and engage in a discussion concerning the nature of the statement. Possible statements include:

Boys are stronger than girls.
Girls are smarter than boys.
George Washington was a great president.
George Washington was the greatest president.
January is the coldest month.
Blondes have more fun.
Everyone celebrates the Fourth of July.
Bananas taste better than peaches.

Children can create their own board game on school trivia (28). The game can focus on various categories such as The Playground, The Building, People at School, and School Events. The children explore the school environment to create questions and answers. Example questions include "How many exit signs are in the school?", "How many swings are on the playground?", and "What is Mrs. Anderson's favorite book?" The gameboard can have spaces designed as obstacles and rewards such as, "You forgot your homework, lose one turn," and "Your math work was excellent, move forward three spaces."

Give each child a sheet of paper on which are written several descriptive statements. The children should mingle among themselves to find a different person who fits each descriptive statement. Examples of descriptive statements include:

> Is taller than you.
> Plays soccer.
> Takes piano lessons.
> Has a little brother.
> Loves to read.
> Knows who Opie Taylor is.

On the back of each child, pin the name of another child in the class. The children must determine whose name is pinned to their backs by asking questions that can be answered either by "yes" or "no." Example questions include:

> Am I a boy?
> Do I have blonde hair?
> Do I sit next to Mike?
> Am I taller than me?

Chapter 6

INTEGRATING SUBJECT CONTENT

One afternoon there was a sudden rainshower. It was one of those showers that seemed to appear from nowhere with such power as to distract even the most highly structured, authoritarian classroom. That's exactly what happened in Mrs. Offderhide's room, but she said to her awestruck children, "You've all seen rain before." She then went right on teaching, just as she had done when the geranium on the windowsill died (12).

Next door Ms. Jolley was as excited as the children about the rain. Everyone went to the window to get a better view. Ms. Jolley told the children to close their eyes and listen. Stephanie said that it sounded like "bacon frying in the skillet" and Alan thought it sounded like "a lot of people clapping really hard." They predicted how long the rain would last. Anthony was closest with his prediction of four and a half minutes. The children predicted where puddles would be and where there would be no puddles. When the rain stopped, they went on a puddle expedition. The location and the width and depth of discovered puddles were recorded in the children's science journals.

In today's early childhood classroom the teacher is asked to teach many subjects on a regular basis in addition to numerous isolated units scattered throughout the year. This all must be completed in a limited time period. Integrating subject areas is a very efficient and effective way to present all of the required subject material. The whole-language approach is an excellent method for integrating subject areas through the reading and writing processes (16). The whole-language approach uses common sense, keeping instruction simple and not inhibiting the learner. This approach offers a language-rich environment that can be applied to any subject area in the early childhood classroom.

IDEAS AND ACTIVITIES

Key Elements of the Whole-Language Approach (47)

Reading to Children

Quality children's literature and appropriate materials from various subject areas can be used to present learning experiences on specific topics and to encourage children to read themselves.

Shared Book Experiences

A small-group reading activity, often using Big Books, where children's favorites are read and reread.

Sustained Silent Reading

A time each day when everyone, including the teacher, reads. Reading material is self-selected. The teacher can provide reading material that covers all subject areas or focuses on a timely topic or unit of study.

Guided Reading

Books are assigned to the children individually or in groups, for independent reading. Teacher–child conferences follow the reading. Books can be assigned for independent study of any subject area.

Language Experience

The children's oral language is recorded and put in written form for the children to use. Experience charts or stories can be created following a field trip, a cooking activity, a science experiment, or any other learning experience.

Children's Writing

Children write to communicate, not to make perfectly formed letters in perfectly straight rows. Student-authored books, poetry, and journals are examples of children's writings. Journals can be used in various subjects. Science journals can be used to record hypotheses and results of experiments. Math journals can be used for recording estimates, predictions, and the strategies used for solving problems.

Guidelines for Creating a Whole-Language Environment (18)

The room should be arranged so that all children can be independent learners.

A variety of materials that are easily accessible to children should be provided. The following sections describe a sampling of these materials.

All areas of the room should contain reading and writing materials.

Begin the school year with a limited amount of available materials and gradually add to them throughout the year.

(See Bibliography for further reading on Whole Language.)

Materials to Provide for Specified Areas (18)

The reading area: Carpet or rugs, an easel for Big Books, trade books, a tape recorder with earphones and multiple copies of the story, pillows, and a rocking chair.

The writing area: Tables, chairs, desks, a file box for children's work, various kinds of paper (e.g., lined, unlined, construction, and note), blank books for children to fill with writing and illustrations, envelopes, a stapler, pencils, crayons, calligraphy pens, and a date stamp.

The math area: Along with the traditional manipulatives such as pattern blocks and counting pieces, provide board games, puzzles, paper, pencils, and calculators.

The science area: Materials provided will be determined by the current area of study but standard materials should include the children's science journals, pencils, reference books, and written instructions, questions, and explanations.

Integrating Subject Areas

A scavenger hunt (1) is a good activity for integrating subject areas. The hunt can be done individually or children can be placed in groups for a cooperative learning experience. Children can hunt for things—

- that are the size of a baseball.
- smaller than your foot.
- skinnier than a pencil.
- that are square (or round, rectangular, oval).
- found in pairs.
- that are soft (or hard, smooth, rough, sharp).
- that make noise.
- that are pretty.

Reserve a section of the chalkboard for reinforcing a previously learned concept (M. J. Hattabaugh, personal communication, September 6, 1990). Write a heading on the board such as "Compound Words." At various times during the school day, children can go to the board and add a compound word to the list. All children should be encouraged to participate. The teacher should monitor the answers and discuss any incorrect or questionable answer with the child in a positive way. Other categories could be—

- Words that rhyme with man
- Math sentences that equal ten
- Animals seen on a farm
- Contractions

- Even numbers
- Things a magnet will attract.

In all subject areas, use written instructions and questions instead of verbal ones and require written responses.

Journals can be included as a regular part of daily writing. The journals can be used as private diaries, for teachers to respond to the children's entries, and for use with science and math activities. For example:

1. Provide materials for a sink-float activity. Have each child study the materials and record in the science journal predictions for what will sink and what will float. Next, the child experiments with each item and records what actually happened. Then the child compares the results to the original predictions, including ideas on why predictions were either accurate or inaccurate.

2. Have children plant a garden, either flower or vegetable. The children should record the date of planting, the watering schedule, and weekly observations. This can lead to experiments with varying the amount of water and light different plants receive. Several plants could be used. A schedule of watering and sunlight should be determined for each plant. Daily observations are recorded in science journals, comparing and contrasting the growth rate of each plant.

3. Have each child hold half of a ruler on a table with the other half extending off the table. The children should then twang the extended end of the ruler. Hard and easy twangs should be used. Adjust the amount of ruler held on the table and the amount extended. The children should record in their journals how the sound of the twang changed with each adjustment.

4. Keep a log of the growth of a class pet.

5. On the chalkboard, draw the pattern (see below) for "Petals Around the Roses" (R. Reed, personal communication, June 3, 1981). Write "How many petals are around the roses?"

above the pattern. Have children write in their math journals what they think is the answer and explain why.

Pattern:

.   .   .   .

    .   .   .

.   .   .   .

Hint: center dots are roses.

    6. Place six milk jugs in a row. The first three jugs are full, the last three are empty. Write this problem on the board: "By moving only one jug, rearrange the row so that full and empty jugs alternate." Children can record strategies, attempts, and possible solutions in their math journals.

    Have children write the words for wordless picture books.

    Provide opportunities for children to write to state agencies, favorite authors, politicians, newspaper editors, travel agencies, and so on.

    Establish pen pals for the children. The pen pals can be in another class in the same school, or in another school in the same city, or even from a different city.

    Children can conduct classroom or school polls and report the results. The polls can focus on environmental issues or events occurring locally, nationally, or internationally. Create a "Meet the Press" or "60 Minutes" program.

    Children can send and decode secret messages using the following code:

	1	2	3	4	5
1	A	B	C	D	E
2	F	G	H	I	J
3	K	L	M	N	O
4	P	Q	R	S	T
5	U	V	W	X	Y
6	Z				

A set of two numbers stands for a certain letter. For example, 21 is B, 35 is W, and 54 is T. And always remember,

21 51   11   34 42 44 13   54 11 13 51 34.

CONCLUDING COMMENT

Most children entering early childhood classrooms are uninhibited and analytical risk-takers. Others are more inhibited. Our goal is to help those natural risk-taking behaviors remain as a permanent part of children's learning styles and help those less willing to take risks regain and rediscover risk-taking.

Teachers who encourage risk-taking to flourish are usually risk-takers themselves. They teach in ways that are best for their children. This involves offering developmentally appropriate learning experiences and opposing outside pressures to push children too fast in order to raise meaningless test scores. Our children and our society desperately need teachers to take the risks to provide this quality education. The purpose of our profession is too important to settle for less.

REFERENCES

1. Adams, Dennis N. "Involving Students in Cooperative Learning." *Teaching K–8* 20, no. 7 (April 1990): 51–52.
2. *An Agenda for Action: Recommendations for School Mathematics of the 1980's*. Reston, Va.: National Council of Teachers of Mathematics, 1980.
3. Barbour, Nita H. "Can We Prepackage Thinking?" *Childhood Education* 65, no. 2 (Winter 1988): 67–68.
4. Barman, Charles R. "Science from the Sponsors." *Teaching K–8* 20, no. 5 (February 1990): 64.
5. Baroody, Arthur J. *Children's Mathematical Thinking*. New York: Teacher's College Press, 1987.
6. Barth, Roland S. "A Personal Vision of a Good School." *Phi Delta Kappan* 71, no. 7 (March 1990): 512–516.
7. Bertrand, Nancy P., and Fairchild, Steven H. "Reading Readiness Through Writing." *Dimensions* 14, no. 3 (April 1986): 4–6.
8. Bloom, Benjamin S., ed. *Taxonomy of Educational, Objectives, Cognitive Domain*. New York: David McKay, 1956.
9. Bruni, James V. "Problem Solving for the Primary Grades." *Arithmetic Teacher* 29, no. 6 (February 1982): 10–15.
10. Carin, Arthur A., and Sund, Robert B. *Teaching Science Through Discovery*. Columbus, Ohio: Merrill, 1989.
11. Carr, Kathryn S. "How Can We Teach Critical Thinking?" *Childhood Education* 65, no. 2 (Winter 1988): 69–73.
12. Cullum, Albert. *The Geranium on the Windowsill Just Died, But Teacher You Went Right On*. New York: Harlin Quist, 1971.
13. Danielson, Kathy E. "Creating Interest in Words with Literature." *Childhood Education* 66, no. 4 (Summer 1990): 220–25.
14. Dewey, John. *How We Think*. New York D. C. Heath, 1910.
15. Duckett, Paula. "Washington,D.C.: Problem Solving." *Teaching K–8* 20, no. 4 (January 1990): 63–65.
16. Espe, Cathie; Worner, Cindy C.; and Hotkevich, Maureen M. "Whole Language—What a Bargain!" *Educational Leadership* 47, no. 6 (March 1990): 45.
17. Faggella, Kathy. "Seasonal Picture Books." *First Teacher* 11, no. 4 (April 1990): 7–9.
18. Fisher, Bobbi. "The Environment Reflects the Program."

Teaching K–8 20, no. 1 (August-September 1989): 82,84,86.

19. Freeman, Evelyn B., and Hatch, J. Amos. "Emergent Literacy: Reconceptualizing Kindergarten Practice." *Childhood Education* 66, no. 1 (Fall 1989): 21–24.

20. Frymier, Jack, and Gansneder, Bruce. "The Phi Delta Kappa Study of Students At Risk." *Phi Delta Kappan* 71, no. 2 (October 1989): 143–46.

21. Goodman, Yetta. "Children Coming to Know Literacy." In *Emergent Literacy: Reading and Writing,* edited by William H. Teale and Elizabeth Sulzby. Norwood, N.J.: Ablex, 1986.

22. Greenes, Carole E., and Schulman, Linda. "Developing Problem-Solving Ability with Multiple Condition Problems." *Arithmetic Teacher* 30, no. 2 (October 1982): 18–21.

23. Hall, Nigel. *The Emergence of Literacy.* Portsmouth, N.H.: Heinemann, 1987.

24. Harste, Jerome C.; Woodward, Virginia A.; and Burke, Carolyn L. *Language Stories and Literacy Lessons.* Portsmouth, N.H.: Heinemann, 1984.

25. Hemmer, Earlene. "Belgrade, Montana: The Role of the Teacher." *Teaching K–8* 20, no. 4 (January 1990): 66–68.

26. Hendrick, Joanne. *The Whole Child.* Columbus, Ohio: Merrill, 1988.

27. Hopkins, L. B. "A PoeTree." In *Pass the Poetry, Please,* edited by H. L. Hopkins. New York: Citation Press, 1972.

28. Kahn, Shirley. "School Trivia." *Teaching K–8* 20, no. 1(August–September 1989): 96.

29. Kamii, Constance, and Kamii, Micko. "Why Achievement Testing Should Stop." In *Achievement Testing in the Early Grades,* edited by Constance Kamii. Washington, D.C.: National Association for the Education of Young Children, 1990.

30. Kennedy, Leonard M., and Tipp, Steve. *Guiding Children's Learning of Mathematics.* Belmont, Calif.: Wadsworth, 1988.

31. Krulik, Stephen, and Rudnick, Jesse A. "Teaching Problem Solving to Preservice Teachers." *Arithmetic Teacher* 29, no.6 (February 1982): 42–45.

32. Lamme, Linda L. "Illustratorship: A Key Facet of Whole Language Instruction." *Childhood Education* 66, no. 2 (Winter 1989): 83–86.

33. Lee, Kil S. "Guiding Young Children in Successful Problem Solving." *Arithmetic Teacher* 29, no. 5 (January 1982): 15–17.

34. Lester, Mary. "Rio Linda, California: A Team Effort." *Teaching K–8* 20, no. 4 (January 1990): 72–74.

35. Leyden, Michael B. "Shadow Watching." *Teaching K–8* 20, no. 1 (August-September 1989): 44–45.

36. ____."An Ice Way to Start the Year." *Teaching K–8* 20, no. 4 (January 1990): 38,41.

37. ____. "Acids, Bases, and Acid Rain." *Teaching K–8* 20, no. 5 (February 1990): 33–34.

38. ____. "Bouncing the Beams." *Teaching K–8* 20, no. 5 (February 1990): 62–63.

39. ____. "Pendulum Pondering." *Teaching K–8* 20, no. 6 (March 1990): 26–27.

40. Luzadder, Valerie M. "Cut Your Class a Story." *Teaching K–8* 20, no. 7 (April 1990): 42–44.

41. May, Lola J. "Estimation: Another View." *Teaching K–8* 20, no. 1 (August-September 1989): 22, 24–25.

42. Moses, Barbara. "Individual Differences in Problem Solving." *Arithmetic Teacher* 30, no. 4 (December 1982): 10–14.

43. Parker, Carol J. "Teaching Young Gifted Children in the Preschool Classroom." *Dimensions* 14, no. 4 (July 1986): 4–6, 25.

44. Polya, George. *How To Solve It.* Princeton: Princeton University Press, 1973.

45. Puckett, Margaret B., and Black, Janet. "Learning to Read." *Dimensions* 13, no. 3 (April 1985): 15–18.

46. Reuter, Janet R. "Island Hopping." *Teaching K–8* 20, no. 5 (February 1990): 55–57.

47. Robbins, Patricia A. "Implementing Whole Language: Bridging Children and Books." *Educational Leadership* 47, no. 6 (March 1990): 50–54.

48. Sandel, Lenore. "What Can a Poem Do?" *Childhood Education* 66, no. 4 (Summer 1990): 210–13.

49. Silverstein, Shel. *Where the Sidewalk Ends.* New York: Harper and Row, 1974.

50. Slavin, Robert E., and Madden, Nancy A. "What Works for Students At Risk: A Research Synthesis." *Educational Leadership* 46, no. 5 (February 1989): 4–13.

51. Stephens, Karen. "Junior Journalists." *First Teacher* 10, no. 10 (October 1989): 4, 13.

52. Sulzby, Elizabeth. "Kindergartners as Writers and Readers." In *Advances in Writing Research* edited by Marcia Farr, Vol. 1,

Norwwood, N.J.: Ablex, 1985.

53. Szabo, Janice A. "Fairy Tales, First Graders, and Problem Solving." *Teaching K–8* 20, no. 6 (March 1990): 45–46.

54. Teale, William H. "Home Background and Young Children's Literacy Development." In *Emergent Literacy: Reading and Writing,* edited by William H. Teale and Elizabeth Sulzby. Norwood, N. J.: Ablex, 1986.

55. Tegano, Deborah W.; Sawyers, Janet K.; and Moran, James D. "Problem Finding and Solving in Play: The Teacher's Role." *Childhood Education* 60, no. 2 (Winter 1989): 92–97.

56. Troeger, Virginia B. "Student Storytelling." *Teaching K–8* 20, no. 6 (March 1990): 41–43.

57. Trostle, Susan L., and Cohen, Stewart J. "Big, Bigger, Biggest: Discovering Dinosaurs." *Childhood Education* 65, no. 3 (Spring 1989): 140–45.

58. Weinstein, Rhonda, and Shein-Gerson, Debra. "Brookline, Massachusetts: Manipulatives in K–8." *Teaching K–8* 20, no. 4 (January 1990): 69–71.

59. Wolfinger, Donna M. "Mathematics in the Preschool-Kindergarten." *Dimensions* 18, no. 1 (October 1989): 5–7.

60. Woods, Donald R. "How Might I Teach Problem Solving?"In *Developing Critical Thinking and Problem-Solving Abilities,* edited by James E. Stice. San Francisco: Jossey-Bass, 1987.

BIBLIOGRAPHY

FUN WITH WORDS

Alexander, M. *Pig Says Oink: A First Book of Sounds.* New York: Random House, 1978.

Aylesworth, J. *Hanna's Hog.* New York: Atheneum, 1988.

Bellamy, J. *The Doubleday Children's Thesaurus.* New York: Doubleday, 1987.

Beller, J. *A-B-C-ing.* New York: Crown, 1984.

Boynton, S. *A Is for Angry.* New York: Workman, 1983.

Burningham, J. *Jangle Twang.* New York: Viking, 1985.

Butterworth, N., and Inkpen, M. *Nice or Nasty: A Book of Opposites.* Boston: Little, Brown, 1987.

Day, A. *Frank and Ernest.* New York: Scholastic, 1988.

Gwynne, F. *The King Who Rained.* St. Louis, Mo.: Treehouse, 1970.

_____. *A Chocolate Moose for Dinner.* St. Louis, Mo.: Treehouse, 1976.

_____. *A Little Pigeon Toad.* New York: Simon and Schuster, 1988.

Hanson, J. *Plurals.* Minneapolis, Minn.: Lerner, 1979.

_____. *Possessives.* Minneapolis, Minn.: Lerner, 1979.

_____. *Sound Words.* Minneapolis, Minn.: Lerner, 1976.

Maestro, G. *What's a Frank Frank? Tasty Homograph Riddles.* New York: Clarion, 1984.

_____. *What's Mite Might? Homophone Riddles to Boost Your Word Power!* New York: Clarion, 1986.

Nixon, J. L. *If You Say So, Claude.* New York: Viking, 1986.

Parish, P. *Amelia Bedelia's Family Album.* New York: Greenwillow, 1988.

Purdy, C. *Iva Dunnit and the Big Wind.* New York: Dial, 1985.

Spier, P. *Fast-Slow, High-Low: A Book of Opposites*. New York: Doubleday, 1972.

____. *Gobble, Growl, Grunt*. New York: Doubleday, 1971.

Terban, M. *The Dove Dove*. New York: Clarion, 1988.

____. *Eight Ate: A Feast of Homonym Riddles*. New York: Clarion, 1982.

____. *I Think I Thought and Other Tricky Verbs*. New York: Clarion, 1984.

____. *Your Foot's on My Feet! And Other Tricky Nouns*. New York: Clarion, 1986.

POETRY

Bennett, Jill, comp. *Tiny Tim: Verses for Children*. New York: Delacorte, 1981.

Blishen, Edward. *The Oxford Book of Poetry for Young Children*. New York: Watts, 1963.

Bodecker, N. M. *Hurry, Hurry, Mary Dear! And Other Nonsense Poems*. New York: Atheneum, McElderry, 1976.

Brewton, Sara; Brewton, John E.; and Blackburn III, G. Meredith. *My Tang's Tungled And Other Ridiculous Situations*. New York: Crowell, 1973.

Ciardi, John. *The Man Who Sang the Sillies*. Philadelphia: Lippincott, 1961.

Cole, William. *Good Dog Poems*. New York: Scribner's 1981.

Cole, William, ed. *An Arkful of Animals: Poems for the Very Young*. Boston: Houghton Mifflin, 1978.

____. *Monster Knock Knocks*. New York: Simon and Schuster, 1988.

Corrin, Sara, and Corrin, Stephen, comps. *Once Upon a Rhyme: One Hundred One Poems for Young Children*. Winchester, Mass.: Faber, 1982.

Farber, Norma. *Never Say Ugh to a Bug*. New York: Greenwillow, 1979.

Ferris, Helen, comp. *Favorite Poems Old and New*. New York:

Doubleday, 1957.

Finlay, Ian Hamilton. *Poems to Hear and See.* New York: Macmillan, 1971.

Frank, Josette. *More Poems to Read to the Very Young.* New York: Random House, 1968.

____. *Poems to Read to the Very Young.* New York: Random House, 1961.

Froman, Robert. *Seeing Things: A Book of Poems.* New York: Crowell, 1974.

Kennedy, X. J. *One Winter Night in August and Other Nonsense Jingles.* New York: Atheneum, 1975.

Kherdian, David. *Country Cat, City Cat.* New York: Scholastic, 1978.

Lewis, Richard, ed. *In a Spring Garden.* New York: Dial, 1964.

Lobel, Arnold. *The Book of Pigericks.* New York: Harper and Row, 1983.

Prelutsky, Jack. *The Baby Uggs Are Hatching.* New York: Greenwillow, 1982.

____. *The Snopp on the Sidewalk and Other Poems.* New York: Greenwillow, 1977.

____. *Toucans Two and Other Poems.* New York: Macmillan, 1970.

____. *Zoo Doings: Animal Poems.* New York: Greenwillow, 1983.

Rimanelli, Giose, and Pinsleur, Paul. *Poems Make Pictures, Pictures Make Poems.* New York: Pantheon, 1972.

Roethke, Theodore. *Dirty Dinky and Other Creatures: Poems for Children.* New York: Doubleday, 1973.

Royds, Caroline, ed. *Poems for Young Children.* New York: Doubleday, 1986.

Strickland, Dorothy S., ed. *Listen Children.* New York: Bantam, 1982.

Untermeyer, Louis, comp. *The Golden Treasury of Poetry.* New York: Golden Press, 1959.

Worth, Valerie. *More Small Poems.* New York: Farrar, Straus and Giroux, 1976.

_____. *Small Poems.* New York: Farrar, Straus and Giroux, 1972.

_____. *Still More Small Poems.* New York: Farrar, Straus and Giroux, 1978.

WHOLE LANGUAGE

Barrett, F. L. *A Teacher's Guide to Shared Reading.* Richmond Hill, Ontario: Scholastic, 1986.

Clay, M. M. *What Did I Write?* Auckland, N.Z.: Heinemann Educational Books, 1975.

Cutting, Brian. *Getting Started in Whole Language.* Auckland, N.Z.: Applecross, 1989.

Goodman, Kenneth S. *What's Whole in Whole Language.* Portsmouth, N.H.: Heinemann, 1986.

Jensen, J. M. *Composing and Comprehending.* Urbana, Ill.: National Council of Teachers of English, 1984.

Kidder, Tracy. *Among Schoolchildren.* Boston: Houghton Mifflin, 1989.

Lamme, Linda L. *Growing Up Writing.* Washington, D.C.: Acropolis, 1984.

Lynch, Priscilla. *Using Big Books and Predictable Books.* New York: Scholastic, 1986.

Moffett, J., and Wagner, B. J. *Student Centered Language Arts and Reading, K–13: A Handbook for Teachers.* Boston: Houghton Mifflin, 1983.

Newman, Judith M. *Whole Language Theory in Use.* Portsmouth, N.H.: Heinemann, 1985.

Peetoom, Adrian. *Shared Reading: Safe Risks with Whole Books.* Richmond Hill, Ontario: Scholastic, 1986.

Watson, Dorothy; Burke, Carolyn; and Harste, Jerome. *Whole Language: Inquiring Voices.* New York: Scholastic, 1989.